SCHOLASTIC

Handwriting Practice
WACKY FACTS

By Violet Findley

New York • Toronto • London • Auckland • Sydney
Mexico City • New Delhi • Hong Kong • Buenos Aires

Contents

Cover design by Judith Christ-Lafond
Interior design by Maria Lilja
Illustrations by Doug Jones

ISBN: 978-1-338-03061-7

1 2 3 4 5 6 7 8 9 10   40   21 20 19 18 17 16

Introduction

Welcome to *Handwriting Practice: Wacky Facts!* In the hustle and bustle of a hectic school day, handwriting often gets short shrift. With reading, writing, math, science, and social studies to learn, few students have the time or inclination to perfect the fine art of crossing *t's* and dotting *i's*. What a shame! Clear handwriting is one of the best tools available to kids for expressing big ideas and showing what they know.

That's where these lively practice pages come in! In as little as five minutes a day, you can spur students to spruce up their handwriting. Just reproduce and pass out a page, then sit back and watch kids move their pencils with levity and care. Why? Because the simple act of rewriting a wacky fact motivates them to master the shape, size, spacing, slant, and curve of model script.

And here's more good news: The completed practice pages can quickly be bound into instant wacky-facts books to share with family and friends. What a cool way to showcase a child's best handwriting!

Read on to discover more tips for using this resource to improve your students' handwriting and, in the process, their essential communication skills.

Your partner in education,

Violet Findley

Using This Resource

This book has been designed for easy use. Before embarking on the wacky-facts pages, it's a good idea to review the basics. Do so by distributing the upper- and lowercase practice pages to students. These sheets include arrows showing the standard way to form each letter. As students complete these pages, circulate around the room looking for writing "red flags"—that is, kids who are forming their letters in nonstandard ways, for example from the bottom up. If you notice an error, approach the student and model standard formation. This will help kids rewire their handwriting habits, which will improve both the clarity and speed of their printing down the road.

Once students have reviewed the basics, they're ready to enjoy the wacky-facts pages. These pages can be reproduced in any sequence you choose. Here are some simple routines for sharing them:

Handwriting Starters Place a practice page on each student's desk to complete first thing in the morning.

Handwriting Center Stock a table with a "practice page of the day" for students to complete independently.

Handwriting Homework Send home a page each night for students to complete independently.

Handwriting Folders Create personal handwriting folders filled with photocopies of the pages for students to complete at their own pace.

Making a Wacky-Facts Booklet

Once students have completed their pages, they can follow these simple directions to make personal booklets. Note: The booklets can comprise as many pages as you like. They need not include every page.

1. Cut the photocopied pages along the dashed lines, discarding the top portions.

2. Optional: Photocopy the blank booklet sheet on page 47 to add original wacky facts to the booklet.

3. Photocopy the booklet cover on page 48.

4. Place the booklet cover on top of the stacked pages in any order you choose.

5. Staple the book along the left-hand side.

6. Color the booklet cover and interior pages.

7. Share the booklet with family and friends.

Name _____

Tip: Look at the arrows to see how to form each letter.

A B C D E F G H I J K L M

N O P Q R S T U V W X Y Z

Use your best handwriting to copy each letter below.

Wow! Wow! Wow! Wow! Wow! Wow! Wow! Wow!

Extra Wacky!

Octopuses have three hearts.

Name _____

Tip: Look at the arrows to see how to form each letter.

a b c d e f g h i j k l m n

o p q r s t u v w x y z

Use your best handwriting to copy each letter below.

Wow! Wow! Wow! Wow! Wow! Wow! Wow!

Extra Wacky!

A woman in Nevada has 32,000 refrigerator magnets.

Tip: Begin letters from the top, not the bottom.

Name _____

Use your best handwriting to copy the words.

kind

sound

cats

Use your best handwriting to copy the sentences below.

Do you know what kind of sound cheetahs make?

These fierce, fast cats chirp like little birds.

CHIRP!

CHIRP!

Wow! • Wow! • Wow! • Wow! • Wow! • Wow! • Wow!

Extra Wacky!

Male ostriches roar like lions.

Use your best handwriting to copy the words.

Do   play   sport

Use your best handwriting to copy the sentences below.

Do you play soccer? More than 240 million people all around the world play this very popular sport!

Tip: Pull the pencil toward the middle of your body when you write.

Extra Wacky!

The first baseball players caught with bare hands.

Wow! * Wow! * Wow! * Wow! * Wow! * Wow! * Wow! * Wow! * Wow!

Name _____

Use your best handwriting to copy the words.

most   are   like

Use your best handwriting to copy the sentences below.

Vanilla is the most popular ice cream flavor. But there are
some other odd flavors to try, like popcorn and hot dog!

Wow! · Wow! · Wow! · Wow! · Wow! · Wow! · Wow! · Wow! · Wow!

_____

_____

_____

_____

_____

_____

_____

_____

Extra Wacky!

It takes 50 licks
to finish an ice
cream cone.

Name _____

Use your best handwriting to copy the words.

Tip: All uppercase letters should touch the top and bottom lines.

wonder

it   ride

Use your best handwriting to copy the sentences below.

Ever wonder what mosquitoes do when it rains? Sometimes one lands on a drop of water and catches a ride!

WHEEEEEE

Extra Wacky!

A mosquito can flap its wings 500 times a second!

Wow! Wow! Wow! Wow! Wow! Wow! Wow! Wow! Wow! Wow! Wow!

Name _____

Use your best handwriting to copy the words.

were

nobody

say

Tip: Lowercase letters *b, d, f, h,* and *l* are tall. They all touch the top line.

Use your best handwriting to copy the sentences below.

When telephones were first invented, nobody was sure how

to answer them. So people would just say, " Ahoy!"

AHOY!

Wow! * Wow! * Wow! * Wow! * Wow! * Wow! * Wow!

Extra Wacky!

More people in the world own cellphones than toothbrushes.

Name _____

Use your best handwriting to copy the words.

new

year

forgot

Use your best handwriting to copy the sentence below.

Millions and millions of new trees grow each year from

nuts that squirrels forgot about and left buried in the ground.

Tip: Lowercase letters *g, p, q,* and *y* have tails. The tails hang down below the bottom line.

Wow! * Wow! * Wow! * Wow! * Wow! * Wow! * Wow!

Extra Wacky!

Closing your eyes can help you remember.

Name _____

Use your best handwriting to copy the words.

old   right   left

Use your best handwriting to copy the sentences below.

In the old days, a pair of shoes didn't have a right and left.

Either foot went inside either shoe. Ouch! Ouch!

Tip: Try to make all of your letters stand up straight.

Wow! Wow! Wow! Wow! Wow! Wow! Wow! Wow!

Extra Wacky!

People take about 3,000 steps a day.

Name _____

Use your best handwriting to copy the words.

brother   sister

of

Use your best handwriting to copy the sentences below.

Do you have a younger brother or sister? A child who is
four years old asks about 437 questions each day.

WHERE? ? HOW? ? WHEN? WHO? ?
WHAT? WHY? HOW? ?

Wow! Wow! Wow! Wow! Wow! Wow! Wow! Wow!

Extra Wacky!

Babies smile 400 times a day.

Name _____

Use your best handwriting to copy the words.

well

old

using

Tip: If you are coming to the end of the line, begin the next word on the following line.

Use your best handwriting to copy the sentences below.

Brush well and enjoy your minty toothpaste. In the old days, people cleaned their teeth using ground up eggshells.

Wow! Wow! Wow! Wow! Wow! Wow! Wow!

Extra Wacky!

Hummingbird eggs are as small as jellybeans.

Name _____

Use your best handwriting to copy the words.

mouse   the   made

Use your best handwriting to copy the sentences below.

The computer mouse was invented in the year 1964.

The very first one was made out of wood.

Tip: Practice writing your letters in the air.

Wow! Wow! Wow! Wow! Wow! Wow! Wow! Wow!

Extra Wacky!

Mickey Mouse was first drawn in 1928.

Name _____

Use your best handwriting to copy the words.

famous

keep

cap

Use your best handwriting to copy the sentence below.

Babe Ruth, the famous baseball player, would keep a chilled
cabbage leaf under his cap to stay cool. Batter up!

Tip: You can
practice writing
your letters in
the sand.

Wow! Wow! Wow! Wow! Wow! Wow! Wow! Wow!

Extra Wacky!

**The first
refrigerators
were more
expensive than
the first cars.**

Name

Use your best handwriting to copy the words.

can

able

rhyme

Use your best handwriting to copy the sentence below.

You can try and try and try, but you won't be able to find

any words that rhyme with orange, purple, or silver.

Tip: You can use a finger to practice writing your letters on your friend's back.

I LIKE ORANGE AND I LIKE ???

Extra Wacky!

The color pink can calm you down.

Name _____

Use your best handwriting to copy the words.

have   call   different

Use your best handwriting to copy the sentences below.

Dolphins have special names for one another. They use different whistles to call to their friends in the ocean.

Tip: You can practice writing your letters with finger paints.

Wow! Wow! Wow! Wow! Wow! Wow! Wow! Wow!

Extra Wacky!

Some parrots can learn more than 1,000 words.

Name _____

Use your best handwriting to copy the words.

Your   better   it

Use your best handwriting to copy the sentences below.

Your sense of smell keeps getting better each year until
age 8. After that, it stays the same for many years.

Tip: Drawing
circles, squares,
and triangles
will help you
write better
letters.

Extra Wacky!

**Right after a big
meal, you hear
less well.**

Wow! Wow! Wow! Wow! Wow! Wow! Wow! Wow! Wow!

Name _____

Use your best handwriting to copy the words.

used   stone

glass

Use your best handwriting to copy the sentences below.

Before there were glasses, people used something called a

reading stone. This round piece of glass made words larger.

Tip: Practice
your handwriting
a little each day.

Wow! * Wow! * Wow! * Wow! * Wow! * Wow! * Wow! * Wow!

**Extra
Wacky!**

**Sunglasses
were invented
about a
thousand years
ago in China.**

Name _____

Use your best handwriting to copy the words.

record

seed

the

Use your best handwriting to copy the sentences below.

The record for spitting a watermelon seed is 68 feet.

That is the length of a yellow school bus!

Tip: Make sure your pencil is nice and sharp before you begin writing.

PTUI!

Extra Wacky!

In strong wind, a dandelion seed can travel 500 miles!

Wow! Wow! Wow! Wow! Wow! Wow! Wow! Wow! Wow! Wow!

Name _____

Use your best handwriting to copy the words.

Sun   huge   million

Use your best handwriting to copy the sentences below.

The Sun is way larger than the Earth. Picture the Sun as a huge gumball machine. A million earths would fit inside it!

Tip: Make sure you have a good eraser before you begin writing.

Wow! * Wow! * Wow! * Wow! * Wow! * Wow! * Wow! * Wow!

Extra Wacky!

It takes eight minutes for the Sun's light to travel to Earth.

Name _____

Use your best handwriting to copy the words.

can

many

even

Use your best handwriting to copy the sentences below.

Cheese can be made from the milk of many different animals.

There is even donkey and camel cheese!

Tip: A clean desktop is the best place to practice your handwriting.

Wow! Wow! Wow! Wow! Wow! Wow! Wow! Wow! Wow! Wow! Wow!

Extra Wacky!

Eating cheese can help prevent tooth decay.

Name _____

Use your best handwriting to copy the words.

person   bulb

dark

Tip: Always try your very best.

Use your best handwriting to copy the sentences below.

Thomas Edison is the person who invented the light bulb.

That's a good thing because he was afraid of the dark!

Wow! Wow! Wow! Wow! Wow! Wow! Wow!

Extra Wacky!

Famous actor Johnny Depp is afraid of clowns.

Name _____

Use your best handwriting to copy the words.

ball

weighs

much

Use your best handwriting to copy the sentences below.

The world's largest rubber-band ball was started in 2004. It has 700,000 rubber bands and weighs as much as an elephant!

Wow! Wow! Wow! Wow! Wow! Wow! Wow! Wow!

Tip: Have a good time! Handwriting is fun.

Extra Wacky!

The smallest camera is the size of a grain of salt.

Tip: Begin letters from the top, not the bottom.

Name _____

Use your best handwriting to copy the words.

amazing   fish

and

Use your best handwriting to copy the sentences below.

Eels are amazing! These long, skinny fish have special skills,

like tying their bodies in knots and swimming backwards.

Wow! * Wow! * Wow! * Wow! * Wow! * Wow! * Wow! * Wow!

Extra Wacky!

Kangaroos can't walk backwards.

Name _____

Use your best handwriting to copy the words.

your   one

trick

Use your best handwriting to copy the sentences below.

Can you touch your tongue to your nose? Give it a try!

Only about one in ten people can do this nifty trick.

Tip: Pull the pencil toward the middle of your body when you write.

Wow! Wow! Wow! Wow! Wow! Wow! Wow!

Extra Wacky!

You blink about 25,000 times a day!

Name _____

Use your best handwriting to copy the words.

was   president

any

Use your best handwriting to copy the sentences below.

When John Tyler was president, the White House was

crowded. He had 15 children, more than any other president.

Wow! * Wow! * Wow! * Wow! * Wow! * Wow! * Wow!

Extra Wacky!

George
Washington
loved ice cream.

Name _____

Use your best handwriting to copy the words.

world   two

hours

Tip: All uppercase letters should touch the top and bottom lines.

Use your best handwriting to copy the sentences below.

The world record for longest handshake is held by two brothers.

They shook hands for 42 hours and 35 minutes. Amazing!

Wow! • Wow! • Wow! • Wow! • Wow! • Wow! • Wow! • Wow!

Extra Wacky!

The world record for a mustache is 14-feet long.

Name _____

Use your best handwriting to copy the words.

Slow   city   tiny

Use your best handwriting to copy the sentences below.

On your mark. Get set. Slow! The city of Portland, Oregon, has a tiny park that is used for the sport of snail races.

Tip:
Lowercase letters *b, d, f, h,* and *l* are tall. They all touch the top line.

Wow! Wow! Wow! Wow! Wow! Wow! Wow! Wow!

Extra Wacky!
Sweden has rabbit-jumping contests.

Name _____

Use your best handwriting to copy the words.

days   hard

sing

Use your best handwriting to copy the sentences below.

In the old days, kids had to work hard for Halloween treats.

Often, they had to dance or sing to get fruit and candy!

Tip: Lowercase letters *g, p, q,* and *y* have tails. The tails hang down below the bottom line.

Wow! Wow! Wow! Wow! Wow! Wow! Wow!

Name _____

Use your best handwriting to copy the words.

more   used

kids

Use your best handwriting to copy the sentences below.

Tricycles were invented more than 200 years ago.

The first ones were used by grown-ups rather than kids.

Tip: Try to make all of your letters stand up straight.

Extra Wacky!

There are 1 billion bikes on earth.

Name _____

Use your best handwriting to copy the words.

just

dogs

of

Use your best handwriting to copy the sentences below.

Dinosaurs were bothered by pesky fleas just like dogs are.

These were giant fleas with stingers the size of needles!

Tip: Always take your time when practicing your handwriting.

SCRATCH SCRATCH

Extra Wacky!

Blue whales are bigger than the biggest dinosaurs.

Wow! Wow! Wow! Wow! Wow! Wow! Wow! Wow!

Name

Use your best handwriting to copy the words.

are

planets

rains

Use your best handwriting to copy the sentences below.

There are some very strange storms in outer space.

On the planets Saturn and Jupiter, it rains diamonds!

Tip: If you are coming to the end of the line, begin the next word on the following line.

Wow! Wow! Wow! Wow! Wow! Wow! Wow! Wow!

Extra Wacky!
Venus is covered in volcanoes.

Tip: You can practice writing your letters in the air.

Name _____

Use your best handwriting to copy the words.

back   what

like

Use your best handwriting to copy the sentences below.

Drop a super ball and it will bounce back up. Guess what?

Ripe cranberries also bounce like balls. Give it a try!

Wow! Wow! Wow! Wow! Wow! Wow! Wow!

Extra Wacky!

Strawberries are not berries. They are flowers like roses.

Name _____

Use your best handwriting to copy the words.

around

long

very

Use your best handwriting to copy the sentences below.

Toothpicks have been around for a long, long, long time.

How long? The very first ones were used by cavemen.

Tip: You can practice writing your letters in the sand.

Wow! Wow! Wow! Wow! Wow! Wow! Wow! Wow! Wow! Wow! Wow! Wow! Wow!

Extra Wacky!

Cavemen had short lives. Fifteen was an old caveman.

Name

Use your best handwriting to copy the words.

time   any

their

Use your best handwriting to copy the sentences below.

Elephants spend the longest time pregnant of any mammal.

Female elephants carry their babies for two whole years!

Tip: You can use a finger to practice writing your letters on your friend's back.

YEAR 2

Extra Wacky!

A newborn giraffe can stand up after one hour.

Wow! Wow! Wow! Wow! Wow! Wow! Wow!

Name _____

Use your best handwriting to copy the words.

oldest   trees

years

Use your best handwriting to copy the sentences below.

The oldest living things on earth are trees. There are some

ancient trees that are more than 5,000 years old.

Tip: You can practice writing your letters with finger paints.

Extra Wacky!

An alligator can live to be 100.

Wow! • Wow! • Wow! • Wow! • Wow! • Wow! • Wow! • Wow! • Wow! • Wow!

Tip: Drawing circles, squares, and triangles will help you write better letters.

Name _____

Use your best handwriting to copy the words.

celebrate

days   is

Use your best handwriting to copy the sentences below.

There are lots of special days to celebrate! September 5 is Cheese Pizza Day, and July 10 is Teddy Bear Picnic Day.

Wow! Wow! Wow! Wow! Wow! Wow! Wow! Wow! Wow! Wow! Wow!

Extra Wacky!

January 13 is Rubber-Ducky Day.

Name

Use your best handwriting to copy the words.

candy   was   after

Use your best handwriting to copy the sentences below.

What favorite candy was invented in 1908? The lollipop!

This sweet treat was named after a famous racehorse.

Tip: Practice your handwriting a little each day.

Extra Wacky!

Cotton candy used to be called "fairy floss."

Wow! Wow! Wow! Wow! Wow! Wow! Wow!

Name _____

Use your best handwriting to copy the words.

may

simply

tickle

Use your best handwriting to copy the sentences below.

You may be a little ticklish or a lot ticklish. But either way,

it is simply not possible to tickle yourself.

Extra Wacky!

Very few people can wiggle their ears.

Wow! Wow! Wow! Wow! Wow! Wow! Wow! Wow!

Name _____

Use your best handwriting to copy the words.

sport

moon

hit

Use your best handwriting to copy the sentences below.

Golf is the first sport to be played on the moon. An astronaut

hit a golf ball there, and it glided slowly through space.

Tip: Make sure you have a good eraser before you begin writing.

Wow! Wow! Wow! Wow! Wow! Wow! Wow!

Extra Wacky!

The Earth has earthquakes and the moon has moonquakes.

Tip: A clean desktop is the best place to practice your handwriting.

Name _____

Use your best handwriting to copy the words.

fins   by

only

Use your best handwriting to copy the sentences below.

Swim fins were invented by Ben Franklin when he was only 11 years old. Ben thought swimming was great exercise!

Wow! Wow! Wow! Wow! Wow! Wow! Wow! Wow!

Extra Wacky!

The television was invented by a 14-year-old boy.

Tip: Always try your very best.

Name _____

Use your best handwriting to copy the words.

park   looked

very

Use your best handwriting to copy the sentences below.

One of the first roller coasters looked like a park bench on wheels. There was no seatbelt because it moved very slowly.

Wow! Wow! Wow! Wow! Wow! Wow!

Extra Wacky!

Japan has a roller coaster that you ride using a special bike.

Name _____

Use your best handwriting to copy the words.

number   is   write

Use your best handwriting to copy the sentences below.

Googol is a number. It's way bigger than a million. You write

a googol with a 1 followed by one hundred zeros.

Tip: Have a good time! Handwriting is fun.

Wow! Wow! Wow! Wow! Wow! Wow! Wow! Wow!

Extra Wacky!

Octuplets means eight kids born at the same time.

Blank Booklet Page

Photocopy this page and cut along the dashed line to make an additional booklet page.

Booklet Cover

Photocopy this page and cut along the dashed line to make a booklet cover.